Book design and character illustration by Moran Reudor

ISBN: 979-8-9879291-0-0 (paperback)
ISBN: 979-8-9879291-1-7 (hard cover)
ISBN: 979-8-9879291-2-4 (ebook)

First Edition March 2023

Published by Entirely Whit, LLC
www.entirelywhit.com

To you, my fortuitous village, those old and new, with newfound wisdom & acceptance.

To you, my love, with gratitude.

To you, my inner child, with love.

I Am Good

positive affirmations for children and youth

Written by
Whitney Crawford, LCSW

Illustrated by
Moran Reudor

I am good. I am good. I am good.
I am happy. I am loved. I am bright.
I am good. I am good. I am good.
I am smart. I am kind. I am polite.
I am good. I am good. I am good.

My presence is such a delight.

I am good. I am good. I am good.
I am on purpose. I am forgiving. I am brave.
I am good. I am good. I am good.

I am more than wonderfully made.

I am good. I am good. I am good.
I am outstanding. I am witty. I am cool.
I am good. I am good. I am good.

I will never be anyone's fool.

I am good. I am good. I am good.
I believe. I achieve. And I win.
I am good. I am good. I am good.

My might comes from powers within.

I am good. I am good. I am good.
I am bold. I am fierce. I am great.
I am good. I am good. I am good.

I learn when I make mistakes.

I am good. I am good. I am good.
I rise above. I spread cheer. And I soar.
I am good. I am good. I am good.

I AM CONFIDENT, HEAR ME ROAR!

I am good. I am good. I am good.
I am sincere. I never fear. I excel.
I am good. I am good. I am good.

When you look in my eyes, you can tell.

I am good. I am good. I am good.
I am determined. I am beautiful. I am true.
I am good. I am good. I am good.

I believe in me, and I believe in you.

I am good.
I am good.
I am good.
I am sophisticated.
I am motivational.
I am inspiring.
I am good.
I am good.
I am good.

I welcome you to awe
and admire me.

I am good. I am good. I am good.
I am creative. I am considerate. I am good.

But for some reason, I'm still misunderstood...

We are good. We are good. We are good.
We are happy. We are loved. We are bright.
We are good. We are good. We are good.
We are smart. We are kind. We are polite.
We are good. We are good. We are good.

Our presence is such a delight!

We are good. We are good. We are good.
We are on purpose. We are forgiving. We are brave.
We are good. We are good. We are good.

We were more than wonderfully made!

We are good. We are good. We are good.
We are outstanding. We are witty. We are cool.
We are good. We are good. We are good.

We will never be anyone's fool!

We are good. We are good. We are good.
We believe. We achieve. And we win.
We are good. We are good. We are good.

Our might come from powers within!

We are good. We are good. We are good.
We are bold. We are fierce. We are great.
We are good. We are good. We are good.

We learn when we make mistakes!

We are good. We are good. We are good.
We rise above. We spread cheer. And we soar.
We are good. We are good. We are good.

WE ARE CONFIDENT, HEAR US ROAR!

We are good. We are good. We are good.
We are sincere. We never fear. We excel.
We are good. We are good. We are good.

When you look in our eyes, you can tell.

We are good. We are good. We are good.
We are determined. We are beautiful. We are true.
We are good. We are good. We are good.

We believe in us, and we believe in you.

We are good.
We are good.
We are good.
We are sophisticated.
We are motivational.
We are inspiring.
We are good.
We are good.
We are good.

We welcome you to awe and admire thee.

We are good. We are good. We are good.
We are creative. We are considerate. We are kin.
We are good. We are good. We are good.

We will happily, remind you again.